the Happiness Habit

Daniel O'Leary

First published in 2015 by Columba Press
55A Spruce Avenue
Stillorgan Industrial Park
Blackrock
Co. Dublin
Ireland
www.columba.ie

ISBN: 978-1-78218-255-9
Second Printing

Set in Klinic Slab Book 10/14 and Handsome Script
Book design by Helene Pertl | Columba Press
Printed by L&C Printing Group, Poland

The front and back cover image depicts the Kerry mountain called
'The Two Paps' or, in Irish, 'Dha Chich Anainn', in honour of the Celtic
Mother Goddess Anu, also known as Danu.

IMAGE CREDITS

Front cover painting by the Kerry artist Mary G. Sheehan

Paintings by Micheál O'Leary on pages vii, 2, 8, 12, 18, 24, 30, 34, 36,
44, 48, 52, 62, 64, 66, 74, 82, 86, 90, 92, 96, 98, 104

Photographs by Gerry Symes on pages iv, 6, 20, 22, 26, 32, 38, 40,
46, 50, 56, 58, 68, 76, 78, 80, 84, 88, 94, 100, 102, 106, 114/115

Photographs by Madeleine Fitzpatrick on pages 4, 10, 14, 16, 28,
42, 60, 70

Painting by Mary G. Sheehan on page 72

Contents

Introduction

Let today be the beginning of your new life. From this moment you are already starting on the path of growing and healing, already accepting the invitation to live more fully, to become the unique person you were called to be – your True Self.

You will soon notice the new freedom and energy in yourself; in your thinking, your work, your relationships, your health – even your wealth! You will also realise that you can become more fulfilled than you ever imagined! Another way of living opens up for you.

This small book was written to help you live deeply, to think positively, to find a new hope, to make sense of your suffering, to put a daily spring in your step. It is about turning your life around. You do not have to be a victim any longer of your emotions, family, childhood, religion, your past or present thoughts.

Keep this little book close to you always. Its wisdom will refresh your mind every day. You can start anywhere. But the reading is not for mere information. It is for going deeper into your heart rather than staying on the surface, about changing the way you think, about learning to grow even in your hardest times. The greatest threat to your happiness is the unaware, unlived life.

These pages will also remind you of your role in the grand scheme of things, of your special place in the family of all life since time began. Knowing your True Self means reflecting on your beginnings – long before you were born! You are the child of a most loving universe, chosen by the Mother of Life, given a unique responsibility for the flourishing of your own heart and of the earth itself.

Do not rush the readings. There's one for every week of the year. They gather up the wisdom of centuries. Your heart, in its own time, will recognise and welcome the wise words that nourish it. And then it will dance with a new confidence. It will bring you safely home to that place of happiness within you. Please remember that the courage and trust you need is already there, waiting to be discovered. This small book is to remind you of that!

And then there will be times when, in turn, your friends, your family may look to you for your guidance and healing wisdom. You will have so much to tell them! May the blessing of a happier life be yours – every step of the way.

Part one

THE FIRST HABIT FOR A HAPPIER LIFE:
FINDING AND LOVING YOUR TRUE SELF

The happiness you seek is already within you.

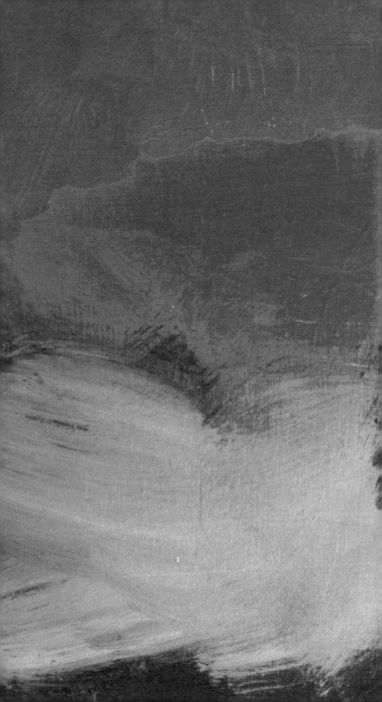

THE AIM OF YOUR LIFE IS TO BE TRULY YOURSELF, FULLY ALIVE AND GRATEFUL

To live out your most precious dreams, to blossom into the best possible version of yourself, to grow into your full power, to find your own voice and to use it – that is the purpose of your whole life, the reason you were created. In the end, that is what good teaching, good parenting, good friendship, good religion and good art are about – to convince you of the beauty of your own 'wild and precious life', and of how to make it flourish. To be fully alive is the greatest gift you can give to yourself, and to the universe. 'Don't ask what the world needs. Ask yourself what makes you come alive and then go and do that. Because what the world needs is people who have come alive' (Howard Thurman). Take a moment now to ask yourself what makes you feel alive.

To thine own self be true, and it must follow, as the night the day, thou canst not then be false to any man.

WILLIAM SHAKESPEARE

Do you believe that? Really believe it? That your first
and only responsibility is to be your authentic self?
Treasured beyond measure, you are the shining image
of your Creator. All you are called to be is what you
are meant to be. Have you noticed something within
you always urging you to be your True Self? You are
forever surrounded by, and filled with this attraction to
something greater and deeper, to a more beautiful way
of living. This healing light shines even in your dark
days. It may not always feel like it but it is there! Once
you try to accept the truth of who you really are, you are
already well on your way to wholeness and happiness.
But you are asleep. 'O terrible human blindness,' wrote
John of the Cross, 'So great a light about you and you do
not see it!'

Nothing can dim the light which shines from within.

MAYA ANGELOU

Your wounds, in the long run, can make you stronger.
Is your current suffering healing you or damaging you,
making your heart stronger or weaker? Life breaks all
of us, but many learn to grow at the broken places.
The place of the wound is the place of healing. Learn
how to turn the stumbling blocks of your life into
stepping stones to your new freedom. A huge secret of
happiness is knowing how to accept, to use and thus
transform your pain, your humiliations, tensions, and
past injustice. If you resist, deny and fume in angry
emotions, you will stay stuck in narrow ways, victimised
by your own thoughts. This is not going to be easy.
Loving your wounds is a tall order. Yet every world
religion, every wise counsel, places the cross of suffering
at the centre of its teaching about acquiring a happier
heart.

*Is not the cup that holds your wine the very cup that was
burned in the potter's oven? … look deep into your heart
and you shall find it is only that which has given you
sorrow that is giving you joy.*

KAHLIL GIBRAN

Fear is a crippling thing; it diminishes your mind and body; it shrivels your soul. Do you want to live in fear or in freedom? Everyone is afraid to some extent. Fear is an intrinsic part of being human. But be aware of its subtle power. Do not attack, avoid or try to banish your fears; meet them, accept them – and you will slowly transform them. They hold the key to your new purpose. Make frequent attempts to do what you fear most, to move outside your comfort zone, and then notice how strong you feel. Remember, most fear is imagined: F.E.A.R. – False Evidence Appearing Real. It takes daily courage to achieve this huge blessing, to live your life fearlessly. Begin taking the risk today – just one small, bold word or action! Try always to speak and act out of your true essence rather than your false ego.

Do the thing you fear and the death of fear is certain.
RALPH WALDO EMERSON

5

Your heart is great. It is made to bless and encourage. It has immense power – more than you ever dreamed of. But you must take care of it. If you are always critical and complaining you become that kind of person yourself. It gets you nowhere. People avoid you. Have you noticed that so many of your thoughts and emotions are repetitive, mostly negative and self-destructive? Avoid judging, blaming, resenting, brooding – negative emotions drain your soul. Celtic wisdom and Gospel guidance remind you that what you give out you get back threefold! Do you praise more than you criticise? Do you forgive more than you resent?

Rake the muck this way; rake the muck that way; it will still be muck. Instead, start dancing your life thankfully on this beautiful earth?

HASIDIC WISDOM

You must continue to believe you have that special, personal spirit within you, a power you can feel and trust, that you can talk to, that will guide and support you, so as to make that important choice each morning. You are searching for more joy in your life. To be glad to be alive is a blessed beginning. To have a thankful heart is a supreme gift. To know that you can grow in all situations – whatever happens, whoever you may meet – is half the battle. To have an abiding sense of wonder about everything that's going to happen today is such a saving grace. Imagine for a moment how well the day will unfold. Every breath can be another new beginning, because at every breath you can choose happiness. There is nothing you cannot do, or be, if you have the courage to believe it.

I can do all things in him who makes me strong.

ST PAUL

It may be just as you wake up, or last thing at night,
or in the middle of the day – but those few minutes of
stillness will eventually bring you a blessed peace. They
will detox your soul, giving you healthy space and vital
energy. Before tidying up the kitchen, checking your
emails, making that phone call or shopping list, stop for
a moment, breathe mindfully. The more you practise it,
the easier it becomes. Simply be still, notice your frantic
thoughts and feelings, relax your shoulders, become
aware of your regular breathing. Even some of the
busiest young professionals take a few minutes every
day for focused conscious breathing, the most effective
way to stay aware, balanced, calm, sensitive. Stillness is
the key. Begin with 5–10 minutes today.

We can make our minds so like still water that beings
gather about us so that they may see, it may be, their
own images, and so live for a moment with a clearer, with
a fiercer life because of our quiet.

W.B. YEATS

LETTING GO IS THE KEY TO HAPPINESS

This is the secret of growing, of happiness, of feeling free: letting go of the desire to be in control, to be always right, to have the last word, to be better than others. It is only by stripping yourself of the useless, non-essential baggage of your life that you can live more happily. You grow by subtraction. Happiness is about letting go. If you learn to drop old resentments, old jealousies and old scores, all things negative and diminishing, you will gradually grow into your True Self. The secret of your new journey lies in the ability to disarm the insecure, possessive ego that we all struggle with. However, the struggle has to be repeated every day. There is no once-for-all magic wand! And only you yourself can do it. Happiness is an inside job! You have what it takes. Just imagine your future!

Most of our troubles are due to our passionate desire for and attachment to things that we misapprehend as enduring entities.

DALAI LAMA

9

Nearly everyone is affected by regrets and guilt about the past, by anxieties and concerns about the future. Very few live in the *here* and *now* – the only real place of happiness. The secret of a healthy mind and heart, according to Buddha 'is not to mourn for the past, worry about the future, or anticipate troubles, but to believe in the present moment, wisely and earnestly'. When you come to your actual physical senses at this moment – what you see, hear, feel – and try to stay with them, you cannot fall into depression or despair. The present is the only place to follow your dream, your passion, your heart. It is the only place of true encounter with people, with life's Creator; the only place to start being your True Self. It is your real home, the safest place from which to begin – now.

So many conditions of happiness are available – more than enough for you to be happy right now. You don't have to run into the future in order to get more.

THICH NHAT HANH

10

Most of your thinking is making you unhappy. It is contaminated! This fact surprises people. You pick and rake over old sores almost every day, scratching at the scabs of past hurts until they bleed again. You rush to conclusions, placing the most negative meaning possible on what happens to you. You forget that the main cause of your unhappiness is not the situation itself, not the things in themselves, not the events that happen, but the way you think about them. You see things, not as they are, but as you are! Do not let your thinking victimise you. This hurting habit accounts for the vast majority of your stress. Check it out with yourself. Becoming aware of it, and then changing this habitual thought pattern will spare you much pain. But it takes time! Do you have the patience to persevere?

We see things, not as they are (objective, impersonal, non-judgemental), but as we are (anxious, vulnerable, very unsure).

21

PRACTISE THE ART OF LIVING MINDFULLY

You become what you think! Are you aware of what's going on in your mind? Is it calmly focused and grounded in the present, or jumping around like a grasshopper? Are you tuned in to what is happening around you, noticing things, aware of what your senses are telling you? Not always easy to do at the beginning, this is a skill you will eventually acquire. Are you trying to be truly present to those you are with, present to all your surroundings? Do you eat mindfully, walk, touch and look mindfully? Do you listen carefully to others, without interrupting their story? Are you one of those sensitive people with a thoughtful, care-filled attentiveness and respect that make others feel safe, un-judged? Such mindful people are daily trying to find, nourish and live out their True Self.

When the mind calms it can hear more subtle things – that's when your thinking slows down, your intuition starts to blossom and you see things more clearly in the present. This is a discipline and you have to practise it.

STEVE JOBS

❊ 12 ❊

You may not know it, but thinking constantly about something – good or bad – is drawing that situation into your own experience. There is a law that orders every moment. There is an extraordinary power in your thinking, in the images of your mind. That is how you attract the light or the darkness into your heart. Your thoughts become your reality! This 'law of attraction' will give you what your thoughts are focusing on. So be careful! Winston Churchill said that day by day we create our own universe. Your life, your happiness, is in your hands. No matter what may have gone before, you can now change every situation in your life. Jesus says that whatever you ask for in true prayer, you are already given, even before you ask for it. What you think about, pray about, you bring about.

Think powerfully, positively and confidently. Once I knew only darkness and silence – before my heart leaped to the rapture of living. Your life will unfold for you as you expect it to.

HELEN KELLER

13

Do you realise the gifts you have within you, what makes you special? Do you ever, for instance, try to name those hidden gifts? What are they? Cooking, decorating, writing, acting, singing, playing, gardening? By not nurturing them, not using your own authentic voice, you will diminish your energy, your mood, your well-being. It is the full, abundant life that you aspire to – not the half-life. When you believe in yourself, there is nothing you cannot achieve, no sadness you cannot transform. Go deeper into that secret place and discover your true and personal power. There is a silent voice in there waiting to speak, to sing; a dance waiting to be danced. Of that you can be sure! But when will you let the voice, the dance, the music out? Today?

The more you enjoy and celebrate your gifts, the more gifts there are to enjoy and celebrate.

OPRAH WINFREY

No matter how well you look, how fine your words and deeds may be, when your heart is angry, bitter or fearful, that is what those around you will catch off you. People will feel the jealousy, the desire for revenge from you, even though you try to hide these destructive emotions. Because such thoughts can be toxic they damage the hearts of others. But first they poison your own soul. What you do not transform you transmit. You prepare for the journey to a happier life by nourishing your heart with truth, beauty and love, by filling your soul with forgiveness and letting go, by choosing to become the authentic person you were created to be. Then those you meet will catch off you, not fear, but energy; not darkness, but a special kind of light. Test this out; notice when it happens.

O Loving Being help me to spread your beauty everywhere I go today. Flood my soul with your spirit and light. Fill my whole being so utterly that all my life may be a radiance of you.

JOHN HENRY NEWMAN

❖ 15 ❖

Everyone has 'dark days' – days when you do not love yourself and feel that no one else does either. You doubt their affection for you. But those who truly love you are not put off when you are down, awkward, feeling inadequate. They notice and delight only in your courage when you face fear, your ability to find the light in your darkness, your hope when things do not look so good. Treasure these people; they are like human angels to support you in your struggle. Because of them your heart will learn again how to play, how to wonder, how to live freely, how to begin anew. Then tomorrow it will be your turn to help them. Just sit down for a few minutes today, close your eyes and let the faces of those precious friends – past and present – pass slowly, gratefully across your mind's eye.

Those true and special friends are the Great Spirit's angels of healing for you, for the peoples of the earth, for the earth itself.

NATIVE AMERICAN WISDOM

Some of your losses and bereavements are almost unbearable. It is important to mourn those losses, and to do it often. Give yourself permission to do this. There are sacred temples that open only to tears. Your greatest heroes and heroines were never slow to express their grief. They often felt a deep anger. Give voice to your own loss and anger. You weep now so as to make way for happiness later. The storms of loss make the trees of your soul grow deeper roots. In the middle of your night of grief a healing dawn will comfort your new day. You cannot detour around your grief; you can only struggle through it, mindfully. Let your healing nature have its way. Look in the mirror today; it will show you a whole and healthy person coming through the dark tunnel of grief.

In the middle of my winter I found an invincible summer.

HENRY DAVID THOREAU

17

You are made for love; always looking for it, always needing it, always wanting to give it. Yet it is already inside you. And around you. People forget that. Why do you block that love from flowing into you, flowing out of you, lighting up your face, giving a spring to your step? Why do you choose to begrudge, to criticise, to be negative? You are created to be the face of love. The Spirit of Love itself has no other way to spread self-belief and courage to all you meet. Do you suspect how precious you are to Life, to your Creator? 'You are God's poetry, written not with ink, but with the love of the Holy Spirit; not on tablets of stone, but on the pages of your heart' (St Paul). Sink yourself into the ocean of that Big Love; trust it, surrender to it. This is the advice of all the Great Wisdom Traditions.

You are created to love and to be loved; to know and to be known; to trust and to be trusted; to hold and to be held. Alone, and in a lonely straight line, nobody goes very far.

ANTOINE DE SAINT-EXUPÉRY

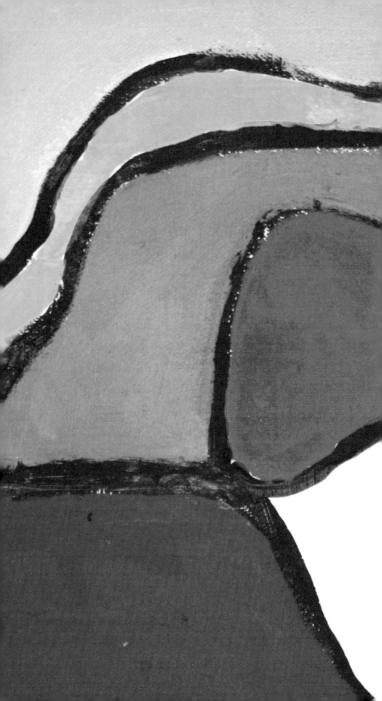

18

Forgiving someone who has hurt you, forgiving yourself, forgiving God, may be the greatest struggle you will ever undertake. The weak can never forgive; forgiveness belongs only to the strong. It is also one of the quickest ways to happiness, to a breathtaking freedom. You cannot be happy while resentment or revenge keeps draining the lifeblood of your heart. It has been said that when a person sets out on a journey of revenge they must bring two shovels – to dig two graves! Resentment is like a cancer that eats away at your soul. It is one of the biggest blockages to your happiness. Forgiving is not about forgetting, or being religious; it is about healing your own heart. You are never more your True Self than when you forgive. Is there someone just now who silently needs your forgiveness? Yourself?

You diminish yourself when you withhold forgiveness. Resentment is a cancer of the soul. If you want to look good, bright with health, forgive everyone. It is the best beauty-treatment!

JACQUELINE BISSET

There ... back ... the source,
ought be nothing more than a teardrop
squeezed from a curlew's eye
then follow it down to the full-throated river
mouth ... a dipper strolls the river
dressed for dinner in a white bib.

The unbroken thread of the beck
... with its nose for the sea
all flux and flex, soft-shaping a pebble
for thousands of years, or here
after hard rain, sawing the hillside in h...
with its chain. Or here, where water unbi...
and hangs at the waterfall's face, and
lost for the one, stretched white moment
becomes lace.

The mind, the heart, the body, the soul – ideally
they all work together. Too often you see them as
separate – some you ignore, others you overindulge.
For any increase in your sense of well-being, all four
need to interweave in a deeper harmony. This harmony
is what defines your personality, your character, the
power of your unique presence. Striking a balance is
the best formula for a happy life. Even after volumes of
recent research into mindfulness techniques, emotional
intelligence, diet and exercise control, and various
spiritualities, the simple wisdom of our childhood days
still holds – all things in moderation, and a healthy mind
in a healthy body. To achieve this state of all-round
balance, a serious commitment and a daily discipline
are needed.

*Happiness is when what you think, what you say, what
you feel and what you do are in harmony. Always aim at
a conscious rhythm and balance, and everything will be
well.*

MAHATMA GANDHI

20

Try to get to know yourself better. Explore your life.
Until you do, you must remain stuck in your old mind.
Self-knowledge is not easy to achieve. You carry
the history of your ancestors within you. Weird and
wonderful characteristics of those who went before
you have come together in you. These include great
darkness and great light, many gifts and many strange
shadows. So have great patience with yourself. Life is
extremely complex. Very few things are certain. Or black
and white. You hear many different voices from your
deepest core. They all belong to you. But one voice only
will be the voice of your True Self. In your stillness you
will hear that inner voice. Trust it and it will see you
through the doubts, defeats and disappointments that
life unavoidably brings.

*The intuitive mind, heart and voice are sacred gifts; and
the rational mind is a faithful servant. We have created a
society that honours the servant-mind and has forgotten
the intuitive gifts.*

ALBERT EINSTEIN

Happiness comes from accepting yourself as you are – the shadow and the light, the sins and the graces, the negative and the positive, the broken parts and the whole. Within every heart there are angels and demons dancing together. On this side of the grave they can never be separated in you, or in those around you. Remember these words in Kahlil Gibran's *The Prophet*, 'The deeper sorrow carves into your being, the more joy you can contain.' In this life you will never become perfectly happy. But the beautiful happiness that you can achieve lies in the knowledge and acceptance of the whole of yourself, warts and all. You are only called to be authentic, to be true to your unique self. You will find many moments every day to try this out! The art lies in recognising those moments.

Joy and sorrow – they come together. When one sits alone with you at your table remember that the other is asleep upon your bed.

KAHLIL GIBRAN

22

Most self-sufficient people find it hard to be vulnerable, to express neediness, to admit feeling lost. Especially men. Behind the bravado you may find a frightened wee boy. To love someone is to be vulnerable. The strong macho man seems too perfect to be weak, and so to be lovable. If you dare to love be prepared to grieve. Your heart will certainly be wrung, and probably broken if you commit yourself to loving someone or something. Do not risk loving if you want to keep your heart safe! So often those we admire are vulnerable people who have succeeded in loving totally. You will never be happy if you are afraid to give your heart away. Our vulnerability makes us open to pain – but also to compassion, to happiness, to healing and fulfilment. It is the surest way to living out your True Self.

The heart of the truest lover, the greatest leader, the purest god, is the flesh of vulnerability.

CHIEF DANCING FISH

23

Without community there can be no real individual fulfilment. People need people. It takes a village to raise a child. Nothing can replace the sense of belonging, in city or country, when you feel part of your environment – knowing the neighbours, supporting your team, campaigning for a good cause, sharing responsibility for the local environment, canvassing for a new leader. When Louis Armstrong saw 'friends shaking hands, saying "how do you do"' he believed they were really saying 'I love you'. A happier life cannot be ordered online. In a sense it is all so ordinary. It silently happens when you are doing other things – taking time to encourage a fearful soul, raising money for people with disabilities, trying to alleviate the burden of poverty, comforting a distressed neighbour.

I do not know what your destiny will be, but one thing I do know: the only ones among you who will be really happy are those who have learned how to serve. This is the only worthwhile life.

ALBERT SCHWEITZER

24

You have a mystery about you that must be carefully looked after. You carry a powerful image of strength and beauty in your heart. Take great care of it. It can be damaged by careless, manipulative hands. So do not let all your sails out to the wayward winds. Do not trust the 'wrong' people with your special secrets. Look for a true companion – your *anam cara*, a 'soul-friend' who will never deceive you, flatter you, or wish for anything but your happiness. Like a wise guardian angel, your 'soul-friend' will not judge you, will stay with you, will reveal to you your true colours. You are rich indeed if you possess a special friend like that. Without having someone to trust with your secrets, to reflect your own life back to you, the journey to wholeness, to your True Self may be impossible.

A person without a soul-friend (anam cara – a true and trusted friend) is like a body without a heart.

ST BRIGID OF KILDARE

25

Learn to keep all your thoughts in the positive energy-field of Love, of Life itself. Become Love so that people can catch it off you! Your unlimited energy, your sense of well-being, your positive approach to every challenge in your life, the very 'who-ness' of your True Self will attract people, opportunities, experiences that never before seemed possible. But you must first open yourself up to the fire of infinite Love in the Spirit of the Creator of all things, in the core of the Earth and in your own heart of hearts. In the conscious energy and flow of this fire you are very powerful. Decide to live like this every day. Christians, for example, put it this way – 'I can do all things in the Spirit who empowers me. I can work all the miracles that Jesus did – and even more!' But do you believe it?

Let yours be great and courageous souls. Always keep your heart big and open to Love.

POPE FRANCIS

26

Happiness grows from the wholehearted acceptance of all that cannot be changed in your life, all that has already happened, all that will inevitably happen. A happier life does not necessarily mean possessing the best of everything but making the best of everything you are and have. Happiness is not about avoiding pain but about how to accept the reality of suffering. So much of your misery arises from wishing that something bad had never happened. Necessary acceptance is not a passive resignation; it saves your precious energy for creative living. Actress Jane Fonda said, 'You don't learn from your successes: you don't learn from your celebrity awards: you only learn from the wounds and mistakes and failures that you cannot change.'

Grant me the serenity to accept the things I cannot change; the courage to change the things I can; and the wisdom to know the difference – living one day at a time …

REINHOLD NIEBUHR

Love is at the core of everything, the very nature and
flow of life. It gave birth to the universe; it sustains it
in its evolution; it will gather all things together at the
end. It draws, drives and empowers the journey of your
life. It is both personal and cosmic, infinitely caring
of both the smallest insect and the whirling galaxies.
Unknown, unknowable, incomprehensible, it is beyond
all religions, churches and creeds. It is deeper than your
deepest breath, wilder than your wildest imagination. It
flows between the words of this 'little book' and between
the beats of your heart as you read it. It is the essence
of everything and everybody; it is infinitely greater
than all creation. Does it have a name? Yes, hundreds of
them – but what is important is that you fall in love with
one of them

Part two

THE SECOND HABIT FOR A HAPPIER
LIFE – RECOGNISING AND NOURISHING THE HEART
OF LOVE IN YOURSELF AND IN ALL CREATION

*If the doors of perception were cleansed everything
would appear to man as it is, infinite. For man has closed
himself up, till he sees all things through narrow chinks of
his cavern.*

WILLIAM BLAKE

1

Many of you will remember those childhood warnings about 'playing it safe', 'keeping your head down', 'knowing your place', 'kicking for touch'. But becoming your True Self demands a daily openness to change, and a daily trust in the Higher Spirit that guides all your aspirations for wholeness. 'Above all,' choreographer Martha Graham told her dancing students, 'keep the channels open.' Like second nature you will then seek to be creative, to risk failure, to persist in beginning again. Do something each day that scares you! The possibilities are many; but costly. Nothing as important as a happier life comes cheaply. There is no point in making it sound easy. It takes, in fact, a total commitment, a kind of dying. You have come this far; why turn back now?

Passion, permanence, perseverance and persistence, in spite of obstacles, discouragements and impossibilities; this is what distinguishes the strong soul from the weak.

THOMAS CARLYLE

Do you barely glance at life as you rush through it? Or do you really see what's going on around you? Truly seeing something reveals all kinds of hidden wonders. Even in the ordinary and mundane. A chance meeting, an argument, a mistake, a boring person, a hurt – each may contain an amazing truth for you. Soon you will learn that everything has some wisdom to give you – if you are really present to it. But first you must take time to recognise the gifts and wonders in your own heart despite its occasional darkness and doubt, its fears and failures. Many people lose heart because of low self-esteem. Like a small angel, that's where this little book comes in – to reassure you of the loveliness of your True Self. In the words of Eleanor Roosevelt, 'No one can make you feel inferior without your consent.'

Trust yourself. Create the kind of self you will be happy with all your life. Make the most of yourself by fanning the tiny sparks of possibility into flames of achievements.

GOLDA MEIR

3

There is so much loveliness in the world to delight in, if you only have the eyes to see it. Especially in those daily, routine moments. The extraordinary is found only within the ordinary. 'It is very simple,' wrote Antoine de Saint-Exupéry: 'It is only with the heart that one can see rightly.' This is a skill that will change your life. Wisdom, enlightenment, grace are everywhere. You can learn so much from a worry, a weed, a word, a wrinkle. The Creator, the Mother of Life, comes to you disguised as yourself, your life, your own experiences. Even in the severe, unavoidable pain of most people, even in the evil within human hearts, in the desperate plight of refugees and migrants, in the wars around the world. How can this be? We do not really know. It is a mystery we struggle with. But we do know that there is no life, no love, no beauty without suffering, and that the Mother, Lover and Healer of Life never deliberately sends any pain or punishment to her beloved family of all creatures.

There's beauty in light; there's beauty in darkness. Beauty is not something extra; for those who can see, it emerges from the deepest mystery of every creature.

CELTIC WISDOM

For some reason people struggle to believe that the
Great Mystery (often called God) is immediately
available and accessible. Many were brainwashed into
believing in a person 'out there' somewhere who keeps
his distance, who judges, who punishes, who allows bad
things to happen to good people. If you believe in this
kind of terrible tyrant you will never be happy. Such
a monster does not exist. The true Giver of Life is, in
fact, in love with you, intensely present wherever you
are working, playing, creating – at your desk, in your
kitchen, your car, checking your smartphone, arguing
about the remote control, rehearsing with the choir,
shopping at Tesco and drinking down at the pub. Like a
star-crossed parent, the Mother of Life loves looking at
you, and delights in you at every moment.

*God's desire is to totally overwhelm you with love; to
have you experience it to overflowing; to have you sense,
feel, taste, and touch his love for you. He really wants you
to experience him.*

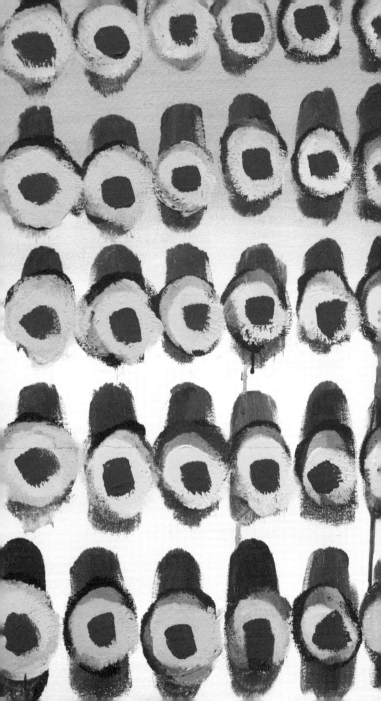

5

The way to happiness will always take you deeper into things. Learn to look at the caterpillar and see the butterfly; to look at the apple seed and taste the ripe apple; to look at death and see new life, to look at the sinner and see the saint. Every thing, place or person is like a small light that shines out an Unconditional Love. This Love is available and accessible in all your daily moments – in your breathing, your heart's beating, your morning chit-chat, your work, your mistakes. Many religions tell us that this Loving Mystery is at the heart of the world, has entered into the human condition with all its sin and shadow, and is now present here and everywhere, delighted to be right in the middle of your own heart and soul. Are you able to believe that you are so loved, so special?

God is not far away from us, distant from the world we see, touch, hear, smell, and taste. He is at the tip of my pen, my spade, my brush. By doing what I do I lay hold of that last end towards which my innermost being tends.

PIERRE TEILHARD DE CHARDIN

When you are truly human you are truly divine. Your
only hope is to be as truly human as you can be. Why?
Because your human presence is the Home of Divine
Presence. Because when you experience true human
love you are also experiencing, and becoming, the Love
of the Creator. They come from the same place – you are
a channel, a reflection, a copy of another beauty. That's
the reason you were created. Even religious people find
it hard to believe that human love is God's love on earth;
that human tenderness is divine tenderness enfleshed
in themselves and in those around them. That is the
reality of the Gracious Mystery. The real presence of the
Higher Love and Power lies in the daily experiences of
human beings. With this way of seeing and of being, you
can always be happy.

*Of one thing I am certain – every human being reveals
something of God … a spark of divine light shines from
each one of us … every human being has been taken up
into the heart of God, conferring on them an infinite
divinity.*

POPE FRANCIS

7

There is a Love-energy within you that makes you blossom, that makes you shine. You already carry the blessed seeds of your own flowering deep within. Every human heart is full of divine promise and power. Your human experiences of joy in your life, courage in your pain, freedom in your fear, letting go in your resentment, staying truthful in a web of lies, fighting depression, staying faithful to your promises, growing younger in spirit as you grow older in years – they are all, somehow, experiences of the infinite Source of Life. When you pause to explore any moment in your days – the bright and dark ones – and sense the Presence of a Greater Love, then you are truly blessed. Your True Self is living out the deep mystery of finding a divine beauty in the most ordinary of things.

It doesn't have to be the blue iris; it could be weeds in a vacant lot, or a few small stones. Just pay attention … (it) is the silence in which another voice may speak.

MARY OLIVER

FIRST YOU LOOK; THEN YOU SEE; FINALLY YOU
RECOGNISE, IN WONDER, THE REAL PRESENCE
HIDDEN EVERYWHERE

Wisdom lies just below the surface of your daily living.
Real living is about going deeper, becoming more
resonant. 'What makes you wise or shallow, sacred or
profane', writes Franciscan Richard Rohr, 'is precisely
whether you live on the surface of things or not.' All
you need, maybe every day, is the reminder, the nudge,
some words from this little book perhaps, to keep you
on your new path of reflecting, being interested, curious
about things. You will need to work at it. Be selective
in the daily paper you buy, the food you eat, the people
you share with, what you watch on TV, the music you
listen to – they are all enriching your imagination or
diminishing it. Look around you, ask questions, go
deeper. Life has been preparing you for this moment
from the beginning of time.

*Look up at the stars, not down at your feet. Try to make
sense of what you see, and wonder about what makes the
universe exist. Be curious.*

STEPHEN HAWKING

All that happens every day is the work and play of the
Gracious Giver of Love, the Mother of Life, the Dance
of the Holy Spirit. When you look long enough at
ordinary events they reveal so much about the Supreme
Artist. Did you know that nature itself has been called
'a mirror of the Maker'? The Creator's fingerprints are
all over the place. Every created thing is there to make
you wonder more intensely – a stone, a river, a bird, an
animal, a human face. When you are living in this way,
every aspect of creation, every genuine laugh or tear,
will be another little book, a love story written for you
by the Great Author. Everyone has the capacity to do
this. After a while, with persevering practice, you will
know that within you, around you, there is – always – a
personal, powerful love.

Too often we are not present to the beauty, love and grace
that brims within the ordinary moments of our lives.
Bounty is there, but we aren't.

RON ROLHEISER

This beautiful line from *Les Misérables* has captivated
the hearts of millions. All true love is divine as well
as human. Your own face reflects the light in the eyes
of the Creator; your heart keeps beating with her/his
energy. You were created to manifest the beauty of
heaven. People can scarcely believe they are made in
the image of a divine Parent; and can experience that
Parent's love in all that happens to them in their deepest
lives. To live is holy; to love is divine; to be is blessed.
'Whatever breaks open the human heart breaks open
the heart of God as well,' a mystic wrote. But it is not
easy to take all of this in, to stay ready and open enough
to this whole captivating mystery. Be patient. Reflect.
To understand this mystery better you will always need
friends around you to share and explore it with.

You were created to be the manifestation of divine
beauty.

THOMAS MERTON

There is a strange reaction in people to good news, to something fine and beautiful, to being set free, to an uplifting vision. Why do people want to stay blind to the love and meaning within them, and all around them? Why is there often a lack of fascination, wonder, delight, curiosity when you hear these marvellous teachings? No one really knows. While good religion helps to set us free from those strange destructive forces that block and blind us to our beauty, bad religion, as so many know to their cost, can utterly distort our capacity for seeing our life in an astonishingly exciting way – both personally and universally. Please give your heart a chance; made in the image of Truth itself, your heart will recognise what will set it free.

The vast majority of human beings dislike, and are even afraid of, liberating ideas with which they are not familiar. That is why prophets are first seen as fools by the fearful.

ALDOUS HUXLEY

12

Does love live at your address? Is it the natural heart of your own family and community? So much creative energy, so many powerful feelings and long-lasting impressions are centred there. It is where you learn the deepest truths of life, by heart; not so much in cerebral lessons as in the way you 'catch' what is enduring and beautiful from those who impress you. Open, trusting, receptive young minds are being daily nourished or damaged by every adult word or emotion expressed in the home and community. Too often there is a terrible adult/parental blindness to the unique mystery of the 'ordinary' family home where life is created, where truth, goodness and faithfulness are reverenced, where love and forgiveness are at the core of everything. But are they?

Perhaps nowhere more than in the heart-felt dynamic of the home – of marriage and family life – where the human spirit stretches itself in its trusting, forgiving and letting go to the limits of its potential, is the expression of true love more clearly lived out. But this is not everyone's experience.

FROM 'IS HOME A HOLY PLACE?'

13

LET NATURE BE YOUR TEACHER; LET YOUR
SENSES BE YOUR GUIDE

Your senses are sacred. When you are mindful of them
they bring you deeper experiences than ever before.
When you listen carefully, you can hear the silent
music beneath the noisy distractions of the day; when
you look with attentiveness, you notice the hidden
loveliness of the most ordinary things; when you touch
someone compassionately, you bless them and yourself
with many graces. Let nature be your teacher. Simply
by watching the sea, the sky, each morning's miracles,
the play of darkness and light, you know you belong to
something bigger. Let your senses teach you that nature
is the first bible. In the turning of the seasons, in the
waxing and waning of each day, nature's allure catches
for you, reveals to you, and stirs within you the strains
and traces of an Astonishing Love.

*May you see what you see through different eyes, hear
what you hear through different ears. May you taste
what you have never tasted before, and go deeper than
your shallow self.*

FROM A MASAI PRAYER

14

There is a place within you called your 'mystical heart'. It is always searching for hidden beauty. It is that part of you that loves to wonder about the meaning of everything – the way things grow, how healing happens, how our bodies work, how our planet turns around the sun, how space seems infinite, how the divine fingerprints are on every particle of matter. Or reflect deeply on how evolution has shaped you, how every cell in your body is a hymn to heaven and a declaration of love. Does your soul delight in recognising the deeper mystery behind the popular TV presentations of scientists and physicists? Your amazing heart is capable of understanding something of this Great Mystery. Nourish it.

The little space within the heart is as great as the vast universe. The Creator of heaven and earth is there, and the sun and the moon and the stars. Fire and lightning and winds are there, all that makes a human being is there …

HINDU SWAMI PRABHAVANANDA

THE UNIVERSE HAS COME FROM ONE SMALL
WOUNDED SEED THAT IS BLOSSOMING
INTO INFINITY

Only in quiet meditation, through contemplative
moments, will you deepen your understanding of
creation, of space, of the cosmos, of the mystery of
your being, of the wound in everything. You will begin
to believe that just as you are, you are a child of the
universe, a unique core of creation, and the stuff of
stars. You have come a long way! Amazingly, everything
is interconnected, all are one – the wounded heart of the
cosmos and the cosmos of your own struggling heart.
When you are in tune with your own pain you are also
in tune with the pain of the universe; in fact it is only
in your evolving, marvellous mind that our planet can
become conscious of itself – its suffering and its joy. A
few decades ago, few of us were aware of how intimately
we are connected with our Mother Earth.

We who are baptised into cosmic evolution, have a
responsibility to evolve and to help this Creation also
evolve towards universal unity.

SR ILIA DELIO

YOU ARE AN INTIMATE, ESSENTIAL PART OF THE
HEART OF LIFE WHETHER YOU KNOW IT OR NOT

All you seek is already within you. You carry your own
river of Love spreading across the fields of Life. We all
flow from the one Source of Being itself. That is where
your power comes from. You are a small flame of the
fire that is Life, that is Love, that is the very Being of
everything. Nourish your heart against the temptation
to despair. Look at a furrowed field after winter's
emptiness, greening with a new sheen of barley; notice
the brave smile on the face of someone touched by
death. You will always be taught and enabled by the
cycle of the seasons, by the Spirit of Life. Think about
these things. Talk about them. Read about them. Tell
these stories to children. After all it is the story of your
life, of theirs, and of this enchanted world. May they
look after her better than we have done.

*Tell every child this: you come out of the energy that gave
birth to the universe. Its story is your story; its beginning
is your beginning.*

BRIAN SWIMME

17

ALONE, AND IN A STRAIGHT LINE, YOU WILL NOT GET VERY FAR

With so much fear and despair in the world, so many evil things happening, you may easily lose heart. You will be tempted to feel sorry for yourself, to settle for less, to go it alone. But think again! This is the time for courage, for hope, for determination. It is the time to lean on your friends, to reach for help, to be openly needy. This is the natural way of restoring your positive energy, your confidence. It is so easy to get depressed. But look around you at all the examples of trust and strength in those you respect and love. And find something uplifting to reflect on: those who trust and believe in you, your special memories, your favourite films and poems, a nature path to walk mindfully with a good friend. In your new wisdom you will quickly regain your essential harmony.

Courage is not about having no fear at all; rather it is about feeling the fear and doing it anyway.

SUSAN JEFFERS

18

Always carry a picture in your heart of what you regard
as beautiful. Your spirit expands when you reflect
on that image. You become like that which you most
admire and desire. When you put all your efforts into
becoming more courageous and free, that is what then
happens! You become what you envisage – the energy
of the dance, the resonance of the music, the call of the
poem, the healing of the touch. Quietly begin this habit
of the heart, this passion for the possible, this trust in
the vision. Begin with the dream. 'If you want to build a
ship', wrote Antoine de Saint-Exupéry, 'don't drum up
people to collect wood and canvas: teach them first to
long for the endless immensity of the sea.' Steer the ship
of your soul by the compass in your heart to your true
north.

What you seek is what you are going to get. What you
expect is what you will call forth and recognise. What you
are ready for is what will come toward you. But it has
to be in you, first, or you won't see it or recognise it even
when it's right in front of you.

RICHARD ROHR

19

All comes from the same Source of Mystery. You carry
the universe in your soul as the universe carries you in
its soul. You are the heart and mind of evolving creation.
After nearly 14 billion years of evolution, humans
are reaching a new level of being, seeing and loving.
Evolution is not some distant background to the human
story; it is your story – the slow, painful love story of
your conception in the heart of Love. Physicist Brian
Swimme wrote, 'We awake to a universe permeated with
love; we spend our time learning how to become this
love.' And Franciscan Richard Rohr believes that 'love is
the energy of the entire universe, from orbiting protons
and neutrons to the orbiting of planets and stars'. And
this indwelling love is a wounded love, forever calling to
us with urgent cries.

*We have to learn this 'new story of the universe'. The
old one is no longer adequate. Science is giving us a
new revelatory experience – a new intimacy with the
earth, bringing it and ourselves into a new order of
magnificence.*

THOMAS BERRY

20

Do you believe that you are unconditionally loved by Love itself no matter what? Allow it to overwhelm you, trusting it for the pure gift that it is. Fragile human love is generally conditional. Unconditional love never judges or wants to change you. It has only your well-being, fulfilment and success in mind. It does not remember your failures, weaknesses, sins. And there is nothing you can do to increase or decrease that love. It is always around you and within you – at the very core of your being. You probably find this difficult to believe. Trust it, and this truth alone will bring you a new courage and freedom. But, as we warned earlier, if you dare to love, be prepared to grieve. Loving and dying. They always go together. And together they change everything.

The beginning of unconditional love is to let those we love be perfectly themselves, and not to twist them to fit our own image. Otherwise we love only the reflection of ourselves we find in them.

THOMAS MERTON

21

The Mother of Creation loves creativity. It is the main reason you were fashioned as you are. It is the Creator's imagination working and playing in you. This creative pulse within you is the pulse of life itself. Scientist Albert Einstein wrote, 'Imagination is everything. It is the preview of life's coming attractions!' So, live your life to the full. Reach out without fearing new experiences. There are so many blessings that only you can offer to others. No matter what your age or path in life may be, it is never too late or silly to develop, even in the smallest ways, the creativity already within you – not for reward or admiration but for your soul to enter a divine dance, to be connected with the heart of life. You will be happiest of all when working and playing with the creative gift of your imagination.

So throw off the bowlines. Sail away from safe harbours. Catch the trade winds in your sails. Explore, imagine, dream.

MARK TWAIN

22

There is always the danger of becoming insular, cut off from others, forgetting that the world is your home, and all its inhabitants your family. When the world is abused, when people are oppressed, then, because all are so intimately connected, all are equally diminished. People are utterly dependent on each other, and utterly responsible for each other. It is simply not possible to be happy while, in selfish indifference, you remain insensitive to the cries of your hungry, exploited, tortured sisters and brothers, ignoring the destruction and plight of the planet you live on. Your renewed concern now for those outside your familiar comfort zone will bring you back to your True Self, in your wider family of all creatures, empowered by the blessings of the Spirit of Life.

All have one Mother, belong to one family, live in the same earthly home. Everyone is responsible to everyone for everything.

FYODOR DOSTOYEVSKY

23

TRUST THE UNIVERSE. ITS SPIRIT IS THE LOVING MYSTERY

This same Spirit is in everyone. It is in everything. It is what empowers you to imagine, to create, to love, to serve. It guides and leads you on your way to a happier life. This readiness, expectation, calls for faith. You have to believe. 'Take the first step in faith,' said Martin Luther King, 'You don't have to see the whole staircase, just take the first step.' Be open to the blessed river of Universal Love. Feel it flow through you. Feel it now. Believe that your life is changing already, even as you read these words. That's what love does. The magnificent universe is constantly contributing to our new freedom. But we need to be always longing for, imagining, anticipating our transformation. Catching your confident desire for happiness, the graced law of attraction will bring all you yearn for.

Spirit is the wellspring of all possibility, the restless pulsation of every movement of Creation and of every desire in the human heart. It is the power of becoming that awakens every stirring of imagination, wisdom and creativity ... And it is present with a cosmic passion and a personal intimacy.

DIARMUID O'MURCHU MSC

24

Whatever you think about, you bring about. Remember to give thanks. Your gratitude gets you involved with the creative energies and frequencies of the universe. Being thankful is such a powerful daily exercise. It lifts you into another place of wholeness. Albert Einstein said 'thank you' hundreds of times each day, especially for the great scientists who went before him. It is important, too, that you have a sense of having already received those blessings for which you ask, and for which you are offering thanks. Visualise the presence of the transformation you desire. This act of imagination sees the change as already happening to you. Mystic Meister Eckhart wrote, 'If the only prayer you ever say in your entire life is thank you, it will be enough.'

Piglet noticed that even though he had a Very Small Heart, it could hold a rather large amount of Gratitude.

A.A. MILNE

❖ 25 ❖

Creation is a web of relationships – a kind of mystical body. Everything in the universe is connected. We are all one, all part of the One Energy Field, the One Creative Source, the One Loving Creator. You, and the Earth you live on, are the Spirit's beauty in matter and flesh. Eternal Love is expressing itself through you, as you and as the world itself. With the Loving Mystery, in stone, star and soul, you are the co-creator of the future. You have the Creator's power to become who you are meant to be, to evolve towards the final 'Omega' of life. Only your fearful, isolated thoughts can disempower you, can cut that vibrant line to your new life. Be ever-ready, expectant, open to the gracious call of the Final Intimacy – now. These empowering teachings and truths will sustain you on your journey.

We all flow from one source. There is a single Creator who remains present to every person and every part of the cosmos, sustaining and empowering their ongoing development. Some will call that process evolution; others the work of the Spirit.

JUDY CANNATO

26

DO YOU BELIEVE YOU ARE MADE IN THE IMAGE
OF THE GRACIOUS MYSTERY; THAT YOU HAVE THE
POWER TO BLESS, TO BRING HOPE, TO TRANSFORM?

As you come to the end of this little book do you see
yourself in a new light? I hope you believe in your
hidden power, your ability to change unjust systems,
within and without, to bring peace where there was
war. That is because your True Self, your deepest
compassionate nature, is already the loving energy
of your Creator. You feel the pain of the world, you
share what you can, you live simply so that others may
simply live. Your very authentic presence will bring
hope to another. And that 'other' may be a suffering
soul a million miles away, a victim of greed, of human
madness. Spiritual teacher Ram Dass wrote, 'We are all
affecting the world every moment, whether we mean to
or not. Our actions and states of mind affect all others,
because we are all so deeply interconnected.'

*A flourishing humanity on a thriving planet rich in
species in an evolving universe, all together filled with the
glory of the Creator: such is the vision that must guide us
at this critical time of the earth's distress.*

ELIZABETH JOHNSON

In the end just four things matter:
How well you have lived;
How well you have laughed;
How well you have learned;
How well you have loved.

Afterword

In seeking to explore the amazing mystery of the
ultimate Love and Meaning at the heart of the universe
and of all created things I have used a number of
interchangeable titles, words and phrases such as
Source of Life, Mother Creator, Tremendous Lover,
Eternal Being, God, Gracious Mystery, etc. All of these
only partially, and inadequately, express the Central
Mystery. But on your journey to a happier life, you need
a strong faith in a Being infinitely greater than yourself.

In a similar way, it is not always easy to meaningfully
write about that innermost space within all of us
where Love lives, enlivening and empowering our
days here on earth. I use words like heart, spirit, soul,
inner self, mystical essence, true self, deepest core,
interchangeably to point towards this inexpressible,
eternal space, this innate capacity within each person.

And also, we struggle to find a way of expressing the
terrible reality of the mystery of evil that is inseparable
from life. I refer to it as a darkness, a pervasive flaw,
an original sin, a human stain, a persistent shadow.
There are perpetrators of evil who, in their violence and

greed are blind to beauty, devastating the planet and its peoples with unrelenting savagery. In the face of this inexplicable human condition there is an ever-present deep distrust, even despair, running through conscious creation that strikes at the heart of our hope. But all the time the light is stronger; and true love changes everything.

I have used all these expressions in a general way to make your journey more sure-footed, to avoid unnecessary confusion and to guard against simplistic certainties. You may have your own words for the above realities. I invite you to focus on what you experienced in your mind and heart while reading these reflections, and to discard any words or images which are not helpful for your understanding just now.

Out of respect for the mystery that you, the reader, are, and for the Spirit that drives and draws you, please read these pages as my very inadequate effort to make some sense of our frail and wonderful world, and of his own 'one, wild and precious life' (Mary Oliver).

The mystical element of every world religion, the wisdom traditions of all great cultures, echo through these pages. For instance, because Christianity insists on a fleshed God, it sees the whole mystery of our lives as an intense personal, cosmic and divine love story (see Pope Francis' Laudato Si', 2015). If you are interested in reading more about these life-giving insights, please check the listed books (overleaf), or visit www.djoleary.com.

Other books by the same author:

Prism of Love (2000)

Travelling Light (2002)

Passion for the Possible (2003)

Already Within (2007)

Begin with the Heart (2008)

Unmasking God (2011)

Treasured and Transformed (2014)

Also, by Redemptorist Press, boxed set of CDs:

Reaching for God's Light (2012)

All books are currently available from The Columba Press.

ACKNOWLEDGEMENTS

Pat Dorrian, Tom Dorrian, Anthea Dove, Madeleine Fitzpatrick, Anne Harding, Teresa Laverick, Linda Marsh, Rose McCrave, Greg McCrave, Eileen McParland, Áine Moynihan, Maura O'Leary, Micheál O'Leary, Celia Sparkes, Gerry Symes and Leonie Davies, for playing their own different parts in getting this work finished. The encouragement, inspiration and love of many friends – all sincere searchers of wisdom and wholeness – have brought these pages to life. Margaret Siberry especially believed in the book's promise and worked so generously to complete it.

Patrick, Helene and Michael of The Columba Press did just about everything possible to craft my dream into this beautiful shape.

My thanks also to those great teachers of life, of humanity, of the earth and of the heavens on whose work this book is based – but only in the light of my own experience and journey. I make huge claims for its quiet power. The good news is that your own holy, human, busy hearts will sense the attraction of the truth and love in the pages before you. Those hearts were created to hear and recognise that attraction. And to know and believe that a happier life can be yours. What is needed now is the wake-up call. 'Don't go back to sleep,' wrote the Persian mystic Rumi, 'The breezes at dawn have secrets to tell you. Don't go back to sleep. You must ask for what you really want. Don't go back to sleep.'

SELECT BIBLIOGRAPHY

Angelou, Maya, *Rainbow in the Cloud: The Wisdom and Spirit of Maya Angelou*, Random House (New York, 2014)

Blake, William, *The Complete Poems*, Penguin Classics (London, 1978)

Boone, Linda, *Intimate Life Lessons*, Morris Publishing (Kearney, 2010)

Brinkman, Rick, and Kirschner, Rick, *Dealing with Difficult People: 24 lessons to bring out the best in everyone*, McGraw-Hill (New York, 2003)

Delio, Ilia, *The Emergent Christ: Exploring the Meaning of Catholic in an Evolutionary Universe*, Orbis Books (Maryknoll, 2011)

Dyer, Serena and Dyer, Wayne, *Don't Die with Your Music Still in You: My Experience Growing Up with Spiritual Parents*, Hay House (Carlsbad, 2014)

Ferm, Deane W., *The Courage of Our Confusion: The Last Hurrah of a Senior Citizen*, Wipf & Stock Publishers (Eugene, 2004)

Gallagher, B.J., *It's Never Too Late To Be What You Might Have Been*, Viva Editions (Berkeley, 2009)

Gibran, Kahlil, *The Prophet*, Vintage Books (New York, 2015)

Grumett, David, *Teilhard de Chardin: Theology, Humanity and Cosmos*, Peeters Publishers (Leuven, 2006)

Hudson, Trevor, *The Serenity Prayer: A Simple Prayer to Enrich Your Life*, Kregel Publications (Grand Rapids, 2005)

Jeffers, Susan, *Feel the Fear ... and Do It Anyway*, Ballantine Books (New York, 2006)

Johnson, Elizabeth A., *Ask the Beasts: Darwin and the God of Love*, Bloomsbury (London, 2014)

Keller, Helen, *Optimism: An Essay*, Kessinger Publishing (Whitefish, 2010)

Marques, Joan F., *Empower the Leader in You! An analysis of the most important factors that distinguish a great leader from an average one*, AuthorHouse (Bloomington, 2004)

Merton, Thomas, *No Man is an Island*, Mariner Books (New York, 2002)

Milne, A.A., *The Complete Tales of Winnie-the-Pooh*, Dutton Children's Books (New York, 1996)

Nieman, Peter, *Moving Forward: The Power of Consistent Choices in Everyday Life*, Balboa Press (Bloomington, 2015)

O'Murchu, Diarmuid, *In the Beginning was the Spirit: Science, Religion, and Indigenous Spirituality*, Orbis Books (Maryknoll, 2012)

Oliver, Mary, 'The Summer Day' in *New and Selected Poems*, Volume One, Beacon Press (Boston, 1992)

Oliver, Mary, *Thirst: Poems*, Beacon Press (Boston, 2007)

Rohr, Richard, 'Seek and You Will Find' in *Richard Rohr's Daily Meditation*, Centre for Action and Contemplation (Albuquerque, 2014)

Rohr, Richard, *Immortal Diamond: The Search for Our True Self*, Jossey-Bass (San Francisco, 2012)

Saint-Exupéry, Antoine de, *The Little Prince*, Egmont (London, 2001)

Savary, Louis M. with Berne, Patricia H., *You are God's Gift to the World: The Purpose of Your Life on Earth*, Balboa Press (Bloomington, 2013)

Swimme, Brian, *Canticle to the Cosmos*, Sounds True (Louisville, 1996)

The Teaching of Buddha, Bukkyo Dendo Kyokai (Tokyo, 1966)

Wiese, Christian M., *The Magnificent Experiment: The Magic of Connecting With Your Tao*, Balboa Press (Bloomington, 2013)

Yeats, W.B., *The Celtic Twilight: Faerie and Folklore*, Dover Publications (Mineola, 2004)